just

THE JOB

& Fashion

00032070

This book is due for return on or before the last date shown below.

3 0 SEP 1999

1 8 NOV 2002

19 Dec 06

*Also published in the **Just the Job!** series:*

Art & Design
Care & Community
Construction & Architecture
Consumer & Home Services
Engineering
Finance & Financial Services
Horticulture, Forestry & Farming
Hospitality, Food, Travel & Tourism
In Uniform
Information & The Written Word
Land & The Environment
Law & Order
Leisure, Sport & Entertainment
Management, Marketing & PR
Manufacturing & Production
Medicine & Health
Motor Vehicles & Transport
Nursing & Therapies
Office & Administrative Work
Scientific Work
Selling, Retailing & Distribution
Teaching
Telecommunications, Film & Video
Working with Animals
Working with the Past
Working with your Hands

just THE JOB

Beauty, Hairdressing & Fashion

Lifetime Careers
WILTSHIRE

Hodder & Stoughton
A MEMBER OF THE HODDER HEADLINE GROUP

Just the Job! draws directly on the CLIPS careers information database developed and maintained by Lifetime Careers Wiltshire and used by almost every careers service in the UK. The database is revised annually using a rigorous update schedule and incorporates material collated through desk/telephone research and information provided by all the professional bodies, institutions and training bodies with responsibility for course accreditation and promotion of each career area.

ISBN 0 340 68794 0
First published 1997

Impression number   10 9 8 7 6 5 4 3 2 1
Year   2002 2001 2000 1999 1998 1997

Copyright © 1997 Lifetime Careers Wiltshire Ltd

All rights reserved. No part of this publication may be reproduced or transmitted in any form or by any means, electronic or mechanical, including photocopy, recording or any information storage and retrieval system, without permission in writing from the publisher or under licence from the Copyright Licensing Agency Ltd. Further details of such licences (for reprographic reproduction) may be obtained from the Copyright Licensing Agency Ltd, 90 Tottenham Court Road, London W1P 9HE.

Printed in Great Britain for Hodder & Stoughton Educational, the educational publishing division of Hodder Headline Plc, 338 Euston Road, London NW1 3BH, by Cox & Wyman Ltd, Reading, Berkshire.

CONTENTS

Introduction	9
Beauty care	11
Beauty consultant	20
Sales demonstrator	24
Retailing	27
Hairdresser	29
Trichologist	37
Wigmaker	40
Beauty & hairdressing jobs on cruise liners	43
Complementary & alternative medicine	45
Alexander Technique. Aromatherapy. Herbal medicine. Naturopathy. Reflexology. Shiatsu.	
Modelling	50
Showroom model. Photographic model. Male model.	
Fashion design	55
Textile design	60
Good at needlework?	63
Fashion/clothing manufacture and other industries using sewing techniques. Fashion and other specialist journalism. Embroidery. Stage and TV costumes. Teaching needlecraft/dress and design. Retailing. Interior design. Dressmaking, alterations, curtain and loose-cover making.	
Working in the clothing industry	69
Designer. Materials buyer. Stockroom worker. Cutter and lay planner. Bundling or dividing. Sewing machinist. Hand sewer. Presser. Examiner. Packing and despatch work. Supervisor. Specialist areas of work.	
Sewing machinist	76

Textiles production 79
Production worker or operative. Craftsman/woman.
Technician. Technologist. Commercial jobs. Design.
Working in the entertainment business 83
Dresser. Wardrobe master/mistress. Wardrobe assistant.
Costume designer. Make-up.
For further information 87

JUST THE JOB!

The *Just the Job!* series ranges over the entire spectrum of occupations and is intended to generate job ideas and stretch horizons of interest and possibility, allowing you to explore families of jobs for which you might have appropriate ability and aptitude. Each *Just the Job!* book looks in detail at a popular area or type of work, covering:

- ways into work;
- essential qualifications;
- educational and training options;
- working conditions;
- progression routes;
- potential career portfolios.

The information given in *Just the Job!* books is detailed and carefully researched. Obvious bias is excluded to give an even-handed picture of the opportunities available, and course details and entry requirements are positively checked in an annual update cycle by a team of careers information specialists. The text is written in approachable, plain English, with a minimum of technical terms.

In Britain today, there is no longer the expectation of a career for life, but support has increased for life-long learning and the acquisition of skills which will help young and old to make sideways career moves – perhaps several times during a working life – as well as moving into work carrying higher levels of responsibility and reward. *Just the Job!* invites you to select an appropriate direction for your *own* career progression.

Educational and vocational qualifications

A level – Advanced level of the General Certificate of Education
AS level – Advanced Supplementary level of the General Certificate of Education (equivalent to half an A level)
BTEC – Business and Technology Education Council: awards qualifications such as BTEC First, BTEC National Certificate/Diploma, etc
GCSE – General Certificate of Secondary Education
GNVQ/GSVQs – General National Vocational Qualification/General Scottish Vocational Qualification: awarded at Foundation, Intermediate and Advanced levels by BTEC, City & Guilds of London Institute, Royal Society of Arts and SCOTVEC
HND/C – BTEC Higher National Diploma/Certificate
International Baccalaureate – recognised by all UK universities as equivalent to a minimum of two A levels
NVQ/SVQs – National/Scottish Vocational Qualifications: awarded by the National Council for Vocational Qualifications and the Scottish Vocational Education Council
SCE – Scottish Certificate of Education, at **Standard** Grade (equate directly with GCSEs: grades 1–3 in SCEs at Standard Grade are equivalent to GCSE grades A–C) and **Higher** Grade (equate with the academic level attained after one year of a two-year A level course: three to five Higher Grades are broadly equivalent to two to four A levels at grades A–E)

Vocational work-based credits	NVQ/SVQ level 1	NVQ/SVQ level 2	NVQ/SVQ level 3	NVQ/SVQ level 4
Vocational qualifications: *a mix of theory and practice*	Foundation GNVQ/GSVQ; BTEC First	Intermediate GNVQ/GSVQ	Advanced GNVQ/GSVQ; BTEC National Diploma/Certificate	BTEC Higher National Diploma/Certificate
Educational qualifications	GCSE/SCE Standard Grade pass grades	GCSE grades A–C; SCE Standard Grade levels 1–3	Two A levels; four Scottish Highers; Baccalaureate	University degree

INTRODUCTION

In this book, we have tried to take the widest possible approach to the jobs in the title. As well as the obvious jobs, such as beauty therapist and fashion designer, you will find a large range of jobs which have a beauty or fashion content. Not everyone who is interested in fashion has the ability or the experience to become a fashion designer. Getting a job in retailing, however, could be an entry to a satisfying career in fashion. The buyers for a big store group are just as influential in the fashion field as designers. They don't need design skills. Experience and a good eye are far more important.

The jobs you will find between these covers are very varied. Qualifications needed can range from nothing at all, up to degree level. Some jobs demand the kind of personality that finds it easy to get on with people; others require the highly creative or, for example with modelling, someone born with the right genes that have given them the looks and height for the job. So, whether you are tall, short, creative, skilled with your hands or have the gift of the gab, there should be something here for you.

BEAUTY CARE

> Beauty specialists work in salons, department stores, health farms and leisure clubs. Other opportunities include work on cruise ships, in salons in hotels and home-visiting services. You can enter training with a few GCSEs, but some courses need A levels or Advanced GNVQ to get started.

There is a wide range of jobs in beauty care: beauticians, beauty specialists, beauty therapists, manicurists, aestheticians, masseurs and masseuses, electrologists ... and so the list goes on! In fact, all these names don't always mean different work. The names of jobs often vary from one salon to another. In addition, there are jobs as sales reps for cosmetic and equipment firms and opportunities in teaching beauty subjects in colleges and private schools.

What beauty care involves
The basic types of beauty work are jobs where you:

- do facial treatments, manicure and pedicure;
- do body treatments;
- do both facial and body treatments;
- just have one or two specific skills – such as manicure, pedicure, artificial nail application, electrolysis, etc.

Which are the best skills to learn?
The first thing people often think of is the make-up and facial side of the work. It seems the most glamorous. But, in fact, it's not make-up but body treatments which are the most important

part of the work in many salons, health farms, and so on. This means things like giving massage by hand and machine, doing electrical treatments, muscle toning and slimming treatments. Hair removal (waxing, epilation or electrolysis) is an important part of both face and body work.

To make sure you get the best chance of employment, it is a good idea to take a training course which covers all aspects of beauty work. This will certainly qualify you for more job openings. It will also be a better basis for setting up your own business, if that's something you'd like to do. If you do decide to specialise in just one sort of beauty treatment, remember that this will limit your career.

A **beauty therapist** is someone qualified to do both facial and body work, while a specialist in facials is often called a **beautician**. Many beauticians take a hairdressing training as well as their facial treatment course, which gives them a wider choice of job. Beauty therapists often broaden their experience by taking courses in things like aromatherapy or reflexology and other 'alternative' medical areas.

What it takes to work in beauty

In some ways, working in beauty is a bit like being a nurse, or doing some other health job. This is because you have to be able to deal with people in a pleasant way, and be sympathetic and tactful. Remember that people often go to a beauty therapist because there's something they don't like about their face or figure. Or it may be because they don't feel confident about their appearance. You can expect two-thirds of your clients to be over 30.

A good beauty therapist must be able to make clients not just look better, but feel better and more relaxed too – this is where the job satisfaction lies. If you work in beauty, you must be well turned-out yourself, of course, or you won't be much of an advert for your profession! A pleasant voice is a big help as well.

You may not realise how much *touch* is involved in a beauty therapist's work. Some people are put off by this when they begin to give treatments, but a beauty specialist must feel happy about close physical contact with strangers. You have to touch people's faces and bodies to do your work, and they may have bad skin, or be fat and flabby!

A full training in beauty therapy is far from being a soft option. It's a difficult course of study on the theory side, and the practical work can be quite demanding and tiring. These days a lot of the heavy massage work is done by electrical equipment, but you still have to spend a lot of the day standing, and some treatments are tiring to perform. What you will be paid varies from one job to another – there aren't any fixed rates.

Ellen – beautician, masseuse and aromatherapist

'I run a beauty clinic in a small town. I work on my own although I do share the premises with a hairdressing salon. This has the advantage of reducing my rent and offering several services to customers in the one place.

I can offer a range of treatments to my clients, including beauty therapy, massage and aromatherapy. I am qualified in all these alternatives that I offer to my customers and I think it is important, in a small town, to have several strings to my bow. I originally trained as a beautician and went on a course later to learn about aromatherapy and massage.

I tend to develop a long-term relationship with my customers and get to know a lot about them.

Having the right kind of personality is very important in this job. People, after all, are very sensitive about both their appearance and their health. I have to be tactful and sympathetic but at the same time give them positive advice. I am always careful to explain to people what a particular treatment involves and what the results are likely to be. It's no good telling someone that massage will cure a badly damaged vertebra, but you can say that the soreness and stiffness will be improved.

I have also to be a good businesswoman. This is a business and I'm everything from finance manager to sales manager and filing clerk. Actually I do share a receptionist with the hairdressing business so that clients can make appointments and be welcomed while I am treating someone else.

This is a demanding business which requires me to be fit and healthy. I'm on my feet all day and massage is really physically quite hard. My fingers are very strong after years of kneading people's backs (I think I could add tearing up telephone directories to my lists of skills!). Also I'm required to work in the evenings and on Saturdays, which can be tough. But I do get a lot of work by offering appointments until 7.30 in the evening which I would otherwise not get.

QUALIFICATIONS AND TRAINING

The usual way to train is by doing a full-time course at a local college or at a private beauty school. In some larger towns, colleges and private beauty schools may run part-time courses in the evenings. That way, you can carry on doing another job while you learn. For school-leavers, employer-based training may be possible. Your careers service will be able to advise you. There may also be ways for adults to train through one of the government's training schemes. Ask at your local adult guidance service/Jobcentre.

You do not necessarily need to have GCSEs or other qualifications to train – but most further education colleges, and many private schools, ask for some passes at GCSE, preferably at grade C or above, or other qualifications equal to these. Your subjects should include English and science. This is because during your training you will learn about things like anatomy, human biology, nutrition and the chemistry of cosmetics and skin preparations. All applicants have an individual interview, when school references or Records of Achievement are taken into account.

Various bodies offer examinations in beauty subjects, and those included here all have reputable qualifications. All the organisations produce lists of colleges which run courses leading to their examinations (see Further Information section).

Courses at local colleges of further education

These colleges mainly offer full beauty therapy courses, which generally last two years full-time. College courses usually lead to NVQs at level 2 or 3. With four GCSEs or the equivalent, there are BTEC National Diploma courses available. You might also take the exams for the Vocational Awards International's various certificates and diplomas in beauty specialisms, such as epilation. A few other independent bodies also offer such course options. You should note that some colleges like students to be at least 18 at the start of certain courses, so check this out locally.

Higher National Diploma courses in Beauty Therapy are offered at a number of colleges throughout the country. The courses cover the whole range of skills and salon treatments of a beauty therapist. They place special emphasis on paramedical and therapeutic aspects, such as remedial camouflage for those with bad scars, birthmarks, etc, sauna treatments and salon management. These two-year full-time courses qualify for mandatory awards. Each has slightly different entry requirements – around the level of four or five GCSEs at grade C or higher, including English and science, plus one A level pass, Advanced GNVQ or a BTEC National Diploma. For full details make your own enquiries to the colleges.

Private schools

There has been a decline in the number of private schools offering beauty and beauty therapy courses. Such courses include very intensive full-time courses, usually lasting about three to nine months. A six-month or nine-month course generally gives a full training in face and body work. Shorter courses and part-time training don't usually cover the full range of subjects. There are also courses lasting only a few days for specialisms such as applying nail extensions, or operating sunbeds.

If you choose a private course, make sure that the school you select has a good reputation. Check that the exams you take are acceptable – colleges where you take outside exams are generally more acceptable than those which only offer their own diplomas. The private schools also offer short courses in specialised areas of beauty work, which can only be taken by people who are already qualified as beauticians and beauty therapists. You could take these later to 'top up' a basic training.

PROSPECTS

Some beauty schools and colleges are able to help present and past students to find vacancies. But you will need to look for jobs for yourself as well. There are specialist magazines which have adverts for this type of work. Job opportunities have been increasing in the past few years, with salons now found even in small towns. But don't expect that it will necessarily be easy to find employment. You may have to move away from your home area for work. When you have some experience and access to capital, you might think about starting up your own salon, or – less expensive – a home treatment service, if there is enough demand in your area.

Adults: most colleges (both public sector colleges and private ones) are keen to have mature students on their beauty courses. You may well find that educational requirements are waived for older applicants. Because many of the clients who go to beauty salons for treatments are themselves middle-aged or older, there are plenty of opportunities for older beauticians and beauty therapists. You need the right sort of personality, of course, and you should be physically fit. As mentioned, you may be able to gain skills and experience in beauty work through one of the government's training schemes.

Other related opportunities
Red Cross Therapeutic Beauty Care Service
The Red Cross trains volunteers in beauty care, to give treatments to patients in medical, psychiatric or geriatric units in hospitals. This is done to give the patients a boost and make them feel better. The volunteers may give them manicures, facials, massages or hair-removing treatments, and there's often a dramatic response. Patients feel cheered up, more confident, more relaxed, and take more interest in their appearance. Treatment is also offered to people in day centres and residential homes.

Volunteers are given training in hand-care, therapeutic beauty care, neck and shoulder and facial massage and light make-up. Their success is judged by continuous assessment, not by exams. This service is run by volunteers only and, while the Red Cross training is not a professional qualification, it could give valuable experience to anyone planning to take a professional training. Get in touch with your local branch of the British Red Cross Society in the first instance, through the phone directory.

Colour analysis/colour consultancy/wardrobe analysis
These are fairly new areas of work, to do with helping people decide which colours suit them best as far as clothing and make-up are concerned.

Choice of colour is very important to the way you look. The right colours can give people a glow; the wrong ones can make them look much older and more sallow than they need to. **Colour consultants** may just choose a range of colours which will make the most of the client's looks. **Wardrobe consultants** also do colour analysis, and then actually go through the client's wardrobe, getting rid of all unflattering garments, and take the client shopping for a new, flattering set of clothes and accessories. Most clients are either people employed in fairly visible and senior jobs, such as business executives and politicians, or women who have a very active social life.

Training is through private courses which tend to last one to three weeks, and appear to be held mainly in the London area. They are fairly expensive and you would have to fund yourself. Job opportunities are either with existing colour/wardrobe analysis companies and franchises, or in self-employment. It's a service for which, outside London, only fairly large cities are likely to be able to provide enough clients. Firms and organisations which offer training courses advertise in beauty and fashion magazines.

TV, photographic and film make-up

There are jobs in the BBC and in independent television companies. The work can involve anything from making up newsreaders, or someone to be interviewed in a programme, to doing elaborate make-up and hairstyles for historical dramas or science fiction series, not to mention horrible wounds and skin conditions for *Casualty* and the like. Only qualified staff are employed, and competition is fierce. Film and Television Freelance Training (see Further Information section) offers a two-year apprenticeship, again only for people who already have hair and beauty qualifications, working with film and television companies. As well as TV and film companies, other areas of employment include make-up for videos, fashion photography and portrait photography. Many make-up artists work on a freelance basis.

There are also some specialist theatrical make-up courses at further education and private colleges, with varying entry requirements. There is an HND in Theatre Design at the London College of Fashion which offers a theatrical make-up option.

BEAUTY CONSULTANT

> Beauty consultants sell cosmetics and other beauty preparations, sometimes demonstrating their products through a free make-up service. They also advise customers on the best use of the products, and need to know how they work and what has gone into the making of them. Academic qualifications are not necessary – your personality and general appearance are more important.

The work is generally in the cosmetics and perfumery departments of fairly large stores and chemists. A beauty consultant may work under contract to a particular cosmetics firm, getting commission on any sales made. It is also possible to work for an agency, doing temporary work when needed – perhaps when regular staff are ill, at Christmas, on exhibition stands, or at sales time.

What the work involves
Besides the selling and advisory work, other aspects of the job might include:

- counter display;
- unpacking deliveries;
- dusting the counter and stock;
- ordering supplies;
- maintaining links with the cosmetics firm;
- travelling around to demonstrate new products;
- organising special sales campaigns and promotions.

Experienced staff may also be involved in:

- managing a small team of consultants, in a large department store;
- training staff.

GETTING STARTED

You are usually expected to have had some full-time sales experience. This should preferably be on the cosmetics counter of a department store or large chemists, but any selling background is very useful.

Most firms have age restrictions. Many like their consultants to be over 18, and some say at least 20, or even older. It may depend on the sort of customer their products are designed for. There isn't an official upper age limit, but staff tend to be in their twenties and thirties.

A few GCSEs at good grades, or equivalent qualifications, are likely to help younger applicants, though exam passes are not essential. Subjects like English, maths and biology are particularly welcomed, and a suitable foreign language if you are working for a foreign firm, or in London and other tourist areas.

What it takes

Beauty consultants need:

- a confident and friendly manner;
- tact and consideration;
- to like people and put them at their ease;
- a good speaking voice;
- a sense of colour and fashion;
- to take a lot of care with their own appearance;
- to be bright, smart and cheerful, even at the end of a long working day;

- to put up with a lot of standing – probably in fashion shoes;
- to withstand a lot of pressure when the shop is busy;
- to accept working on Saturdays – often their busiest day (a day off during the week instead is quite popular with a lot of people);
- to be polite even to the most difficult customers;
- to look smart and well made-up all the time.

Many firms give their staff smart uniforms, free make-up and perhaps other perks such as shoe allowances and dry-cleaning vouchers.

TRAINING

Most large cosmetic manufacturers offer training. They run their own examinations and award diplomas. Training usually covers things like knowledge about the structure of the skin, skin care, make-up, and information about the range of products made by the firm. This may be just cosmetics, but it might include perfumes and hair-care products. Public speaking may also be covered in the training course, if you are going to have to give talks and demonstrations. The initial training courses are quite short, and last just a week or so. Regular refresher courses are held, to keep consultants fully up to date with new products.

A Beauty Consultant's Diploma is offered by the International Health and Beauty Council (see Further Information section). This is usually taken on a part-time basis by people who already have jobs in the beauty business, but is also available as a full-time course. Applicants are expected to have a good basic education and are accepted after a successful college interview. Courses for this Diploma are held at a number of colleges of further education, as well as privately run beauty schools.

National Vocational Qualifications for beauty consultants may become available in the near future. Contact the IHBC for information.

There are also opportunities to work in cosmetics sales in chemists' shops, department stores and other retail outlets, without being a representative for a particular firm.

SALES DEMONSTRATOR

Demonstrators work mainly in shops, supermarkets and department stores. They demonstrate a wide range of items, which can include fashion and beauty products, to customers. They are usually employed by the manufacturer or supplier of the product which they are trying to promote, rather than the stores in which they work. Formal qualifications are often not needed, but a cheerful, outgoing personality is a must.

Manufacturers arrange to promote their products in particular shops at particular times, and find suitable people to demonstrate them. There may be other opportunities at trade fairs or in a mobile display unit, like those double-glazing caravans we've all seen around. Many demonstrators are self-employed or freelance, as employment is generally on a temporary contract.

What it takes
You could be suited to being a demonstrator if you:

- communicate well;
- are enthusiastic, cheerful and polite;
- don't mind standing for hours on end;
- look smart and business-like;
- know all there is to know about your product.

Some demonstrators may have few qualifications, but are able to talk convincingly about the product they are selling. Others may need specific qualifications – for instance, you would expect the person demonstrating a cosmetic product to be a trained beauty consultant or beautician.

TRAINING AND OPPORTUNITIES

Training is usually provided by the firm which makes the product. They will train a demonstrator in selling techniques and teach them about the product. This training may take anything from one day to a few weeks, depending on how technical the product is and whether the job is permanent or temporary.

Some firms will ask for specific qualifications, or they may employ only people with previous experience of shop work.

Wages, conditions and qualifications needed vary a lot from one employer to another. Hours of work are quite likely to be part-time, which is useful for people with family commitments. On the other hand, you will probably be expected to work on Saturdays, when stores are at their busiest. Jobs are likely to be advertised in the local press. Usually you will be paid an hourly rate plus commission, but some jobs pay commission only.

Demonstrating is not a likely job for someone looking for a safe, secure, long-term career. However, it has its attractions if you enjoy meeting people and like variety. There are some opportunities for permanent work – possibly working for a manufacturer or an agency as a senior demonstrator, recruiting and training temporary staff.

just THE JOB

RETAILING

> You could get a job in retailing in any of the sorts of areas of interest explored in this book. There are opportunities in both department stores and specialist shops selling cosmetics, beauty products and fashion accessories.

Jobs such as shop assistant, checkout cashier, warehouse worker or shelf-filler may need a few average GCSEs if you are a school/college-leaver. The more up-market shops tend to expect higher qualifications. To start as a trainee manager, some GCSEs at grade C, or A levels/Advanced GNVQ/BTEC National, will normally be necessary. More and more retail firms are seeking graduates for management training schemes.

You also need . . .
- a neat and tidy appearance;
- a pleasant manner;
- to be polite;
- to be helpful;
- to be good at handling money;
- to be fit – you may be on your feet for long periods, and have to lift and move heavy stock.

Opportunities for mature entrants are generally good. There are many opportunities for part-time work. The number of jobs available depends on the economic climate in the high street.

TRAINING

Most large stores or store groups provide training for their staff. There is initial training at the start of employment, and continual training to keep staff up to date with products and methods. NVQs in Retailing at levels 1 to 4 may be available in your workplace, from operative level to management. Some of the course units relate to various product areas, such as food and fashion.

There are also full-time and part-time courses at colleges of further education, including GNVQ in Distribution at Intermediate and Advanced level. Many schools also offer these courses.

Degrees in distribution or retail management are offered at various universities, although a degree in any subject is generally acceptable for a management career in retailing. There are also various HND (Higher National Diploma) courses in retail and distribution subjects.

You can study on a part-time basis for the examinations of awarding bodies such as City & Guilds, LCCI and Pitmans. As noted above, there are also NVQs at levels 1–4 in Retailing. Ask at your local college of further education for details.

In addition, a lot of specialist qualifications exist. These are offered by various associations and societies which represent particular types of shops. The examinations which they offer test your knowledge of their specialist products. Since knowledge of the goods you sell is important to any kind of retailing, it is a good idea to study for appropriate qualifications if you can. Sometimes there are day or evening classes at colleges of further education to help you, but often you would need to follow a correspondence course.

just THE JOB

HAIRDRESSER

> There are about 30,000 hairdressing salons up and down the country, employing around 150,000 people. Both men and women can train as hairdressers, working with female clients, male clients or both. You can train at a college, or as an apprentice or trainee in a salon.

Hairdressing varies according to the type of salon that you work in, and where it is. In a men's hairdressers, or a salon which attracts elderly customers, you will mostly do traditional styles. But in a city centre salon for young fashion-conscious clients, you will be up to date with techniques to create new looks and styles for all ethnic types. That sort of salon is often unisex, too. Most hairdressing jobs are in salons in town centres and suburbs, but there are occasional opportunities in villages.

Hairdressers cut and style hair, interpreting what the client wants or copying a design from a picture. Cutting is the key to a style. Hairdressers must learn to adapt cuts to suit particular clients. Many clients have their hair cut wet to give a better line, so hair is often shampooed and conditioned before the cut. This may be done by a junior, especially if an experienced stylist is going to do the cut.

Then the hair may be blow-dried, set on rollers or dried using other techniques like 'scrunch drying'. Hairdressers also do perms and straightening treatments, and tint and colour hair. New techniques keep coming along. In a fashion salon, you're learning all the time. In men's hairdressing, beard and moustache trimming are usually offered. Some hairdressers give manicures, too, and fit and dress wigs and hairpieces. These are skilled jobs which need extra training (see next sections).

Hairdressers may also do other jobs in the salon. This is especially likely if it is a small salon without a full-time receptionist or a junior. These jobs include answering the phone and making appointments, receiving customers as they come into the salon, and serving coffee. The salon must always look nice, so there is also tidying and sweeping up, basins to clean, and towels and gowns to be laundered. And, of course, someone has to prepare bills and collect money.

Don't forget hairdressers have a busy day on Saturday, and may also work late evenings. They get time off on other days to make up for this.

What it takes

Qualifications – you don't necessarily need any qualifications to train, but some salons and colleges may ask for GCSEs. Science subjects are useful, together with English and maths. An interest in art is also helpful.

Health and fitness – this is important. Skin allergies are a risk for hairdressers, because of all the contact with shampoo, perm lotions and other chemicals. Breathing troubles such as asthma could be made worse, too. You also need to get used to standing for long periods in a hot, steamy atmosphere. It's very tiring!

Personality – you need to like meeting people. A friendly manner wins a lot of customers. It helps to be a good talker and listener who can make people feel relaxed. You have to keep cool when it's busy, but you must work quickly to get through your appointments on time – the next client won't want to be kept waiting.

Abilities – a good eye for line, form, colour and style is important. It helps a lot if you are interested in fashion, especially if you want to work in a fashionable salon. Obviously, you need to be good with your hands!

Natasha – salon junior in a small hairdressing salon

'When I was little, I always used to go with my mum to the hairdresser's and loved the friendly atmosphere. So when I needed a Saturday job, I managed to get one in the local salon. I didn't mind being the general dogsbody, as there was always something to do, and I liked talking to the customers, especially when they tipped me for washing their hair. I found reception work difficult until I got used to it. I remember one awful day when I had made a mistake with the appointments and two people turned up for the same stylist at the same time. That was the last time I made that mistake!

Because of my Saturday work, I was able to get a training place as a salon junior. I have to go to college one day a week to learn all the stuff you don't have time to learn in the salon, like chemistry and all the different things you can do to hair. It's quite interesting, but I prefer being back at the salon. At the end I will have a National Vocational Qualification level 2 in hairdressing, and then maybe I will be let loose on cutting and styling!

When I'm not shampooing customers' hair, getting the sandwiches, making coffee or sweeping the floor, I get to watch the stylists at work. That's great, as I learn a lot then. When a customer comes in wanting a complete restyle, everyone stops what they are doing to look at the result and see if the customer is happy.'

NATIONAL VOCATIONAL QUALIFICATIONS

The Hairdressing Training Board with the City & Guilds examination board offer nationally recognised qualifications. Hairdressers who take these can be guaranteed to have been properly trained. It doesn't mean that you can't be a hairdresser if you have followed some other training, but having only non-recognised qualifications may make finding a job (or even customers!) much more difficult. To get an NVQ, your salon work is assessed, and you also take written and oral exams.

As a **level 2 NVQ,** the Foundation Certificate in Hairdressing includes the following:

- shampooing and conditioning;
- drying;
- cutting;
- perming and neutralising;
- the basic techniques of changing hair colour;
- salon reception;
- working as a team;
- client care procedures;
- health and safety and salon security;
- using resources effectively.

Optional topics that are also available at NVQ level 2 are setting and dressing, barbering techniques and shaving and face massage.

NVQ level 3 skills build on those of level 2, and cover the creative techniques of the specialist working in fashion hairdressing. This work is covered by the City & Guilds Advanced Hairdressing Certificate course.

For people who run salons, a Hairdressing Management Certificate is available. An NVQ level 4 qualification is being developed.

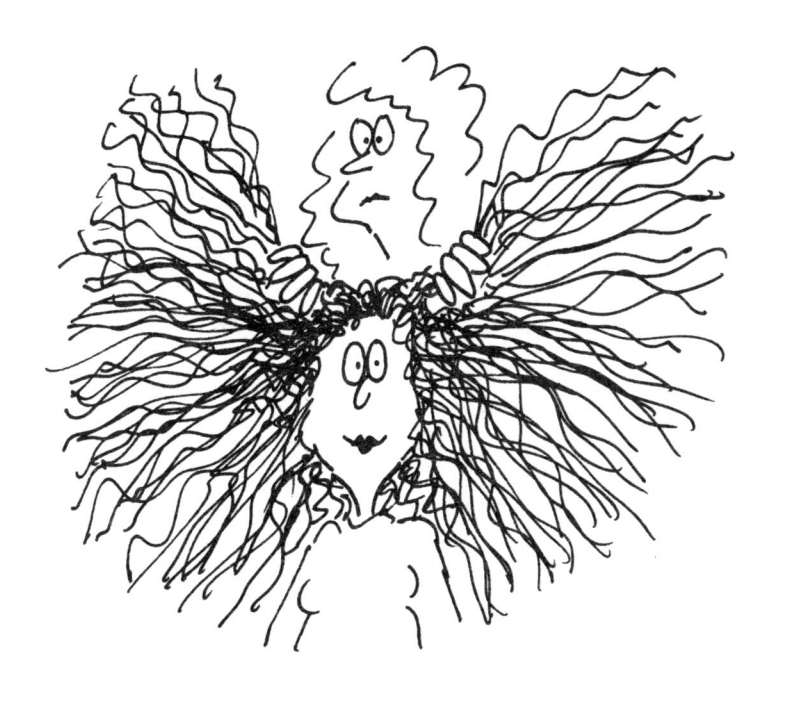

TRAINING

If you are a school-leaver, you can train to be a hairdresser by being based with an employer, such as through an apprenticeship, or you can attend a full-time course at a college or a private hairdressing school. Hairdressing is mainly a young person's career.

If you are an adult, you could train through a course either at a college or at a private school; courses may be offered on a full-time or part-time basis. Government training schemes could also give you a chance of training and gaining NVQs – ask at your local adult guidance service or Employment Services office. Adults could find it more difficult to get a job after training, but self-employment is always a possibility.

Training with an employer

Hairdressing apprenticeships last three years, and normally mean you are based in a salon, working as a junior – learning on-the-job and perhaps going part-time to college, working towards NVQs. Employer-based training, or perhaps a Modern Apprenticeship, may be a possibility in your area. Your local careers service will be able to provide you with further information. Some salons prefer to do their own daytime or evening training. If this is so, be careful – other salons may not recognise it!

Full-time college course

This is the other main way into hairdressing. Hairdressing courses run by local colleges generally last for two years. They usually lead to the NVQ level 2 Foundation Certificate in Hairdressing. To start a course, some colleges may ask school-leavers for a few GCSEs – sciences are useful. Besides courses which are just about hairdressing, there is a BTEC Higher National Diploma in Design (Fashion Styling for Hair and Make-Up) at the London College of Fashion.

Private hairdressing schools

The best-known schools are in London, though there are others around the country. Private schools offer full-time courses for beginners which typically last six months to one year. A lot of training is crammed into a short time. These courses are expensive and you would have to pay for your training yourself. You would have to make sure you were happy about the quality of the training offered.

Courses run by well-known salons are likely to give you a good training, and should offer NVQ level 2 at least. If you choose a private school make sure it is a member of the World Federation of Hairdressing Schools, which is a recognised training organisation. Private schools may also give someone whose main interest is in salon management a level of practical training good enough for their needs. As well as beginners' courses, the private schools run refresher courses and short courses for experienced hairdressers in up-to-date cutting and styling techniques. These can be helpful in advancing your career – a Vidal Sassoon or similar diploma always looks impressive!

Registration

Although not compulsory, only those hairdressers who have obtained NVQ at level 2 are accepted for registration. This registration guarantees an employer or a customer that the hairdresser is trained and qualified. All details can be obtained from the Hairdressing Council.

PROSPECTS

Larger salons and 'chains' have opportunities for senior stylists, managers, and artistic directors to oversee the creative side of the salon's work. 'Chain' or multiple hairdressers are growing. They account for about 20 per cent of salons, and 35 per cent of people working in hairdressing. Wages are notoriously low in hairdressing and many salon employees rely on tips to boost their weekly income.

Self-employment

Once you are trained, you can set up your own salon, if you have enough money and business sense. More simply, you can do this by taking a 'mobile hairdressing service' to customers' homes. Some salons also rent out chairs to stylists, who then work as self-employed people, paying a share of the cost of the bills for heating, lighting, water and so on.

Many colleges offer part-time refresher courses to enable hair stylists to keep up to date with new trends.

Unusual openings
There are some jobs for experienced hairdressers in hospitals, demonstrating for hairdressing product firms, working in salons on passenger ships, hotels, film or TV studios and theatres (see later sections in this book). Huge numbers of people apply for the more glamorous jobs!

Trichology
Some hairdressers decide to specialise in trichology. This means treating scalp and hair conditions – see next section.

Teaching
Another area which *experienced* stylists can go into is teaching hairdressing – in colleges or private schools.

just THE JOB

TRICHOLOGIST

> Most trichologists work in private practice clinics, or in a clinic attached to a hairdressing salon. They work with people who have hair problems, such as thinning hair, and scalp disorders, but they can also work with clients who have healthy hair.

The work of trichologists mainly involves diagnosing hair and scalp conditions and treating them. They use massage, heat and electrical treatments, lotions and ointments, and usually advise their clients on diet and hair care. Clients may come to a trichology clinic directly, or be referred by their doctor or hairdresser.

Some trichologists work in scientific research, or in cosmetic firms or the pharmaceutical industry as consultants in product development.

What it takes

To be a successful trichologist you must be both scientifically-minded and skilled practically, as well as tactful and sympathetic in dealing with people. You may also have to be good at managing your own business affairs. If you intend setting up your own practice or business you will need financial capital.

Getting qualified

Trichology is a small profession, with only about 250 qualified practitioners in the UK – though it is the type of work which is also done by unqualified and not always reputable practitioners.

By law, you don't have to be qualified to practise as a trichologist. But, of course, clients would expect to have their problems treated only by someone with proper training and knowledge, and it is certainly advisable to become properly qualified. Some hairdressers train as trichologists in order to gain an extra field of expertise.

TRAINING

The Institute of Trichologists (see Further Information section) is the professional body, and is concerned to set and oversee standards for the profession. The Institute sets examinations at NVQ levels 1, 2 and 3, for which you would normally study on a part-time basis, by correspondence or through day/evening classes. Students of the Institute must be 18 or over, and have some part-time practical experience, before sitting the level 3 examination.

Colleges currently offering courses in Trichology leading to the Institute's examinations are Clydebank, Belfast and Huddersfield. Part of the training has to be practical at an approved clinical establishment.

You might have difficulty in obtaining a grant from the local education authority to attend one of the courses, so correspondence study is the normal way of becoming professionally qualified in trichology.

Entry requirements for the college courses and the correspondence courses run by the Institute are four GCSEs at grade C, preferred subjects being English, science and mathematics. There can be exemptions from the Institute's examinations for candidates with appropriate qualifications.

GETTING STARTED

Entry to the profession is usually through training with a qualified trichologist. You are advised to train only with a reputable practitioner who has Institute qualifications. You can enter this career as a young person or as an adult.

Trichologists have often previously trained and worked as hairdressers, as might be expected, though the normal work of a hairdresser is, of course, very different from that of a trichologist. Other suitable backgrounds include beauty therapy or an aspect of medical/paramedical work, such as nursing.

Once qualified, there are opportunities in research with pharmaceutical and cosmetics firms as well as in private practice.

just
THE JOB

WIGMAKER

> Wigmakers are involved in making, fitting and maintaining wigs, hairpieces and toupees (small wigs for covering bald patches). Sometimes wigmakers are called **posticheurs**.

Wigs are not only worn by people with little or no hair, but also by actors, entertainers and theatrical artists, lawyers, live models, fashion dummies and sometimes as fashion items. So, some wigs are made up as modern hairstyles which must look undetectable as wigs when worn, whilst others involve historical hairstyles and fantasy fashions. Making legal wigs is a specialism in its own right.

How are wigs made?

Good quality wigs and hairpieces are made from human hair, which is carefully matched for colour and then woven and knotted on to a specially made mount or base. The weaving and knotting of the hair is done either by hand or by machine. You need to be nimble-fingered and patient. It takes a week to put the hair into a single hand-made wig – no wonder they are expensive! Once made, the wig must be cut and styled in the same way as natural hair. Sometimes, nylon is used in place of human hair, while legal wigs are made from horsehair, which is particularly time-consuming to work with.

A dying trade?

There is always a steady if small demand for theatrical wigs, but the demand for naturalistic wigs and hairpieces varies according to fashion trends. At the moment they are not particularly popular. On the other hand, there are always men, women and children who feel they need wigs because they have lost their hair through ageing, chemotherapy or illness. Some clients want a toupee to hide a receding hairline. So there is steady work for skilled wigmakers and dressers.

The job is done mostly in a small factory or workshop, or can even be done from home. The weaving and knotting of wigs is usually done by wigmakers working for small companies. Wigmakers are employed by the biggest theatrical, operatic and film companies, and there is also scope for freelance theatrical wigmakers. There are also specialists in making natural-looking wigs, who have private clients, or clients recommended to them by hospitals if it is felt a wig should be supplied under the National Health Service. Wigmakers are employed by Madame Tussaud's waxworks museum too.

The work doesn't stop once the wig is made – it has to be kept clean, dressed and repaired if necessary. People who wear wigs or toupees all the time need more than one, so that one can be cleaned whilst they are wearing the other. They may also have wigs dressed in alternative hairstyles, too – e.g. for evening wear. Some wigmakers just deal with the making side. Others see the whole process through – measuring, making, fitting, cutting and styling. There is also scope for hairdressers who have been trained in wig and hairpiece work.

TRAINING

The skill is basically learned on-the-job from experienced wigmakers. It takes a good deal of time to become really proficient. Traineeships or apprenticeships are occasionally offered by wigmaking companies and the theatres which employ wigmakers, but it could be difficult finding an opening. Basic wigmaking, fitting, styling and maintenance of wigs can also be studied as part of a college hairdressing and beauty therapy course, though not all colleges offer this option.

There are a number of colleges which offer a City & Guilds 301 course in Wigmaking alone, which can be attended part-time or full-time. See the CRAC *Directory of Further Education* for a list of such colleges, or use the ECCTIS computer database.

Theatrical wigmaking is included amongst topics studied on courses such as the BTEC HND in Theatrical Studies at the London College of Fashion, alongside a general training in theatrical costume or make-up. (Entry requirements for the HND are a minimum of one A level plus supporting GCSEs, or equivalent qualifications – such as BTEC or GNVQ, or relevant prior experience.)

CYRIL USED A TRADITIONAL METHOD OF GATHERING HAIR

just THE JOB

BEAUTY & HAIRDRESSING JOBS ON CRUISE LINERS

> The attractions of working on a cruise liner are obvious. A luxurious ship gliding through warm tropical waters, mooring in exotic ports, moonlit evenings . . . it all sounds very idyllic.
>
> Unfortunately, the crew have to work very hard to make all the delights of cruising available to the passengers! Also, the less desirable cabins are always allotted to the crew – below the waterline, near the engines, no porthole – and you'll probably have to share. Many crew members are only allowed to mix with the passengers on business, so your social life could be limited.

Despite the disadvantages of this sort of life, cruise ship jobs are popular. Competition is fierce, and there are no trainee posts for young entrants. This means that you need to have some relevant shore-based training or experience in the job areas mentioned in previous sections. Employing companies usually expect good qualifications, a few years' relevant experience and the right sort of personality for the unusual life style.

Hairdressers and beauty therapists are usually not employed directly by a shipping line, but by a firm with ship-based salons, such as the maritime division of the Steiner Group. Only very experienced and well-trained therapists and hairdressers will be able to get work on a ship.

FINDING EMPLOYMENT

If you have some relevant experience, write to potential employers asking for information about vacancies. Individual shipping lines should be able to give information about contracting firms providing services for them (see Further Information section).

Overseas Jobs Express, which may be in your local careers service library or public library, is a good source of information about agencies and vacancies for work on cruise liners.

just THE JOB

COMPLEMENTARY & ALTERNATIVE MEDICINE

> The terms **complementary**, **alternative** or **integrated medicine** cover a wide range of treatments such as acupuncture, chiropractic or aromatherapy. Some are based on traditional principles thousands of years old, often emphasising the patient's spiritual health or vitality. Others are more recently developed, and may lend themselves more to scientific appraisal than others.
>
> Treatments are often used *alongside* orthodox medicine, rather than instead of it. The amount of acceptance and recognition gained from the medical establishment varies considerably. Training may involve anything from a five-year full-time degree course to a short correspondence course. Often practitioners in alternative therapies are involved in health and beauty centres and farms.

Practitioners of complementary and alternative medicine or therapies work in private practice, clinics and health farms, and, to a small but growing extent, within the National Health Service. Often people start as assistants in established practices. It can take time to become established. Training can be expensive, although university-validated degree courses qualify you for a mandatory grant. Some professional bodies give loans to set up a practice, and enterprise allowances or career development loans are available to people establishing their own businesses or re-training. Ask at your local Employment Services office.

Most professional bodies suggest that there is an unsatisfied demand for practitioners. Good practitioners need business skills as well as a 'bedside manner'. There may be scope for working abroad, though you would need to investigate the legislation covering practice in other countries.

TRAINING

It is obviously advisable to qualify through a course of training which will be in line with any future national standards. The major therapies are already mostly graduate-only professions, or likely to become so. A system of National Vocational Qualifications is being developed for the less recognised areas. At present these are only available at level 3 in the sort of therapies which are carried out in beauty salons.

Choosing the right course is difficult because of the current lack of national standards. Many registers of complementary practitioners are, in fact, just listings of people who have qualified through a particular college or organisation, which may or may not have been externally examined or be recognised by other bodies. For some alternative practitioners, recognition by the medical establishment is not seen as a priority, and they are quite happy to rely on word-of-mouth recommendation to attract new clients. Many people choose to train in a therapy which they themselves have felt the benefit of, in which case they may be able to take the advice of a practitioner they trust when choosing a course.

Mature entrants are welcomed by training colleges as having more credibility in the eyes of their patients than a younger person would. Often, people qualify in alternative medicine having previously worked in a related job, such as nursing or beauty therapy.

Before committing yourself to any particular non-degree course, you should investigate:

- the appropriateness of the entry requirements;
- the length and thoroughness of the training;
- whether the qualification leads to inclusion on a register and enables you to obtain the insurance necessary to practise;
- the amount of supervised practical experience included;
- whether there is a complaints procedure;
- destinations of previous students and/or evidence of satisfied clients.

Alexander Technique

The Alexander Technique is difficult to summarise, but it is about relearning how to use your body and eliminating the bad postural habits developed over years. Improvement of hand, neck and back coordination generally leads to improvements in physical and mental well-being. Many music and drama colleges have Alexander practitioners on their staff. Training is by a three-year full-time course. No formal qualifications are required. Mature entrants are preferred.

Aromatherapy

This involves the use of aromatic essences extracted from plants to treat a wide range of conditions. The International Federation of Aromatherapists (see Further Information section) has a list of courses which should give access to the British Register of Complementary Practitioners (Aromatherapy Division).

Herbal medicine

Herbal medicine uses remedies from natural plant sources to treat illnesses and correct imbalances in the body.

Middlesex University has a three-year full-time/four-year sandwich/five-year part-time BSc (Hons) degree in herbal medicine which can lead to Membership of the National Institute of Medical Herbalists. Entry requirements are two/three A levels plus supporting GCSEs, including a science. Mature applicants are welcome.

The School of Phytotherapy (Herbal Medicine) offers a four-year full-time BSc (Hons) degree course which requires A levels or equivalent in two subjects, at least one of which should be science-based, preferably biology or chemistry. The School also offers a four-year part-time course of home study with tutorial and practical sessions (satisfactory GCSEs at grade C or equivalent, including English, biology and chemistry, are required). There are also special courses for medical practitioners, and courses in herbal studies for interested lay people, such as those who grow or sell herbs.

The General Council and Register of Herbalists runs a three-year part-time distance learning course with practical workshops and tutorials followed by clinical training. There are no minimum entry requirements. Courses in Chinese herbal medicine and aromatherapy are also offered.

Naturopathy

This is a health-building treatment involving manipulation, diet, hydrotherapy, exercise and a positive philosophy. Four-year full-time courses generally ask for two science A levels from candidates with no relevant experience.

Reflexology

Reflexology involves the application of pressure to specific points on the hands and feet, to release tensions in the body by stimulation of the reflexes. It is designed to relax and balance the body, to improve circulation, and to stimulate the body's own natural healing processes. Training to NVQ level 3 can lead to employment in beauty salons.

Shiatsu

A Japanese traditional treatment, similar to acupuncture except that pressure is used in place of needles. No formal qualifications are required to begin training, but the Shiatsu Society expects people to have trained with a recognised teacher for at least three years, completing 500 hours of study, before being assessed for registration.

just THE JOB

MODELLING

> Models display clothes and/or accessories to the best effect, either live on the catwalk at fashion shows, or in photographs. This used to be predominantly a female profession, but there is an increasing demand for male models. Although modelling seems to be a glamorous, exciting career, only a handful achieve the public image of fame, travel and riches. There are no minimum educational qualifications required, but there are certain physical limitations.

Getting into modelling is very competitive. Only models who are accepted by reputable agencies can expect enough work to make a living, and even this is no guarantee of success. Not all modelling work is glamorous, either. You could be modelling bikinis in Greece one week, but posing in nylon overalls for a mail-order catalogue the next. There are some openings for 'character' models, outsize models, and 'older person' models. Successful models have busy schedules and need to be dedicated and disciplined. However, most models spend a lot of their time unemployed. Modelling is a short career – think seriously about having a second career to fall back on!

What makes a good model?

Have you got the qualities to be a successful model? Are you:

- thoroughly professional and disciplined;
- reliable and punctual;
- adaptable, confident and positive in outlook;
- facially attractive, slim and well-proportioned?

Females starting a career as a model should ideally be aged between 16 and 18, not less than 5 feet 7 to 8 inches in height, and within one inch of 34″–24″–35″. Men should usually be at least 6ft tall, with a 38 to 40 inch chest, 30 to 32 inch waist and 32+ inch inside leg measurement. There are a few openings with agencies specialising in 'characters'.

Showroom model

Showroom models (or 'mannequins') are the only models who are on a payroll. You would work for a fashion house, mostly showing clothes to buyers. To start with, you may have to do some clerical work in the showroom office – invoices, filing, etc. In your first year, you gain valuable experience of the fashion world, employers, showroom work and standards. You should earn enough money to buy the wardrobe of accessories necessary for the next stage of your career – freelance work.

When you are sufficiently well-known and experienced, you'll need an **agent** to get you freelance work in the main twice-yearly fashion shows, when the next season's designs are displayed to retailers, fashion writers, etc.

Photographic model

Models work in various branches of fashion photography, advertising and television commercials (though an Equity card is needed for the latter). Most photographic jobs are not high-fashion, but advertisements for products such as electrical goods, tights and food. Some models just pose where shots of hair, legs, hands, feet, etc, are needed, and make a career from their elegant toes or fingers, or their perfect teeth! It is still essential to have the right proportions overall, though.

Male model

Most of what has already been said applies equally to men and women, though the opportunities may differ. Generally, there are fewer openings for men, though interest in male fashion has widened the scope in recent years. Few men under 30 work full-time in modelling. Men do more 'character' modelling, such as advertising beer or tobacco. Mail-order catalogues and magazines sometimes prefer the more mature, 'rugged' look, so men often have longer modelling careers than women.

Jason – male model

'It's sometimes tough being a male in this business, as most of the work is for females. You really have to make yourself known and push for work all the time, which can be as exhausting as the modelling itself. It's definitely not a job you would do if you didn't enjoy it!

I've just finished a photographic session, which involved wearing a series of ski outfits for what seemed like hours in a hot studio. The photographer just wasn't happy with the lighting. I had to stand in an awkward skiing position for ages, trying to look as if I was enjoying myself in the lovely cold weather. In fact, I was really tired and boiling hot! Still, it was better than another assignment I had, when we had to get up at 4.00 a.m. to catch the sunrise. It was a spectacular sight, but I must admit I prefer my bed at that time of the morning!

This week, I've decided to trail round all the magazine fashion editors in London with my portfolio to try and get myself some more work. Time is running out for me in this business, as I am already 27! That's quite old, even for a male model, unless I decide to stick with the mail-order catalogue work. Ideally, I'd like to run my own model agency one day, but I don't know if I would ever get enough money together for that.'

A modelling course . . . or not?

You don't *have* to take a modelling course, but it can help you to learn the right movements for the catwalk and to get used to being photographed. Take care to pick a reputable school. Most schools will have specific height and build requirements – check individual prospectuses.

Only one state college offers courses in modelling – the London College of Fashion (see Further Information section). Applicants for this one-year full-time course must be over sixteen and preferably with three GCSEs at grade C. All other courses are in private establishments.

Never take a course just because you have at last found a school prepared to take your money! Plenty of people are willing to exploit youthful dreams, and some modelling schools are no more than a racket. Be wary of agencies who insist that you pay for their own schools' courses before putting you on their books. Look carefully at the success rate in employment of past students. Some schools of modelling offer 'grooming' courses lasting a few days – one of these would get you a fair assessment of your chances.

MODEL AGENCIES

You can approach a model agency direct, without first taking a course. The agency will tell you if they think they can find work for you. Send two professionally taken photographs, one of your face and the other showing your shape, to one or more agents, together with details of your age, height and measurements. You can get a list of agents from the Association of Model Agents. Be prepared to be very persistent and, even then, to be disappointed.

Be warned that many agencies deal in models for the less 'respectable' areas of work – e.g. topless or nude 'glamour' modelling.

CARLTON IS MODELLING THE LATEST IN FIRE RETARDANT WEAR

Other points to note

The costs – besides the possible cost of a training course, you will need professional photographs. You will also have to buy your own accessories – shoes, tights, handbags, jewellery, scarves – for photographic sessions. You will also need money to support yourself whilst you get started. Most of the work is in London and Manchester, so you may well have to move. Neither city is cheap in respect of accommodation.

A second career – You should have a second career to fall back on when work is hard to find, or if you are unsuccessful, or when you are older. A skill which can be used in temporary jobs is especially useful.

FASHION DESIGN

> Fashion design is a fast-moving and competitive business, covering footwear and other accessories as well as clothing. Designers must be creative, practical and have a commercial sense. Courses range from GCSE entry up to degree.

Fashion design is perhaps the first career which springs to mind for many people interested in needlework, design and fashion, but it is one of the hardest in which to be really successful.

What it takes

Fashion designers need:

- to be very talented and persevering;
- to be able to imagine a finished garment from a two-dimensional drawing;
- a feel for textiles and their use;
- a flair for creating with fabric;
- to keep up with changes in customer demand and new materials and manufacturing technology.

Designers often have to find sources of fabrics and visit trade fairs to find out about the new designs and products. In small firms, they may do their own pattern-cutting. In larger organisations they work with a team of pattern-cutters and sample-machinists, and with production managers, because production costs influence what the designer can do.

The fashion and clothing industry

The most popular area of work for fashion designers is the dress trade – haute couture, wholesale couture and mass production. To become an haute couture designer, at the very expensive end of the market, is extremely difficult. Most career opportunities are in wholesale and mass production. The amount of creativity expected of a designer varies from firm to firm. In fact, most designers take up and adapt existing fashion crazes, rather than create new trends and styles.

Haute couture

Garments are cut and made individually, to create a new and original style. The designers pay attention to the social habits of their clients, and to the occasions where the garments may be worn. Haute couture includes world-famous designers and firms which design model garments, making the fashion news each season.

Wholesale couture/designer label

Garments are made and sold to retail shops. The designers may follow fashion trends set by the haute couture designers or create their own styles. Many British designers have been successful in this field.

Wholesale manufacture or mass production

Manufacturers produce ranges of clothing and accessories, and supply retail chains, mail-order firms, or produce their own brand names. The processes are mainly automated and controlled by computers. The designer often works within a design team and may also be part of a management team which includes buyers, costing experts, merchandisers and production staff.

Craft and small businesses

There are many small businesses in the clothing industry,

comprising the designer and a partner or small team. The designer designs and organises the production of the merchandise, and may also be involved in marketing and business administration.

Branches of fashion design

Outerwear includes coats, suits, skirts, jackets, trousers, rainwear, etc. This is a specialised and slower-moving area of fashion.

Light clothing includes dresses, blouses, shirts, trousers, separates, evening wear and leisure wear. This merchandise is turned over at a rapid rate, with mid-season as well as main-season ranges.

Children's wear includes specialised firms producing a range of garments, but this is a limited area of employment.

Lingerie, corsetry and swimwear design is a growing part of the fashion industry.

Knitwear is another growing part of the industry, with jobs in firms producing knitwear garments, patterns and wools. Garments may be sold through craft or exclusive designer outlets, as well as being part of most mass-produced ranges.

Accessories includes hats, shoes, stockings, scarves, belts and bags. There are both designer-made and mass-produced products.

Embroidery done by machine is used extensively in the fashion industry for dresses, lingerie and children's wear. Most designing is done by people who have taken special courses in embroidery design at art college.

Theatrical costume design for stage and TV is often a combination of design, dressmaking and historical research. It is a highly competitive field and only the very talented can hope to succeed. Courses are available at a few colleges and drama schools.

> ### Ceri – fashion designer
>
> 'At college I enjoyed both fashion and textile design and found it hard to decide which to specialise in. Textile design is much more varied in some ways, in that it can be about clothes, wallpapers, curtains or flooring, whereas fashion is just about clothes. I eventually chose a degree in fashion because there were more job opportunities in this area.
>
> Fashion design is very much a team affair – I work very closely with the marketing department, the production workers and the retail store buyers, amongst others. We all have our part to play, and have to make sure we talk to each other and listen to each other's point of view.
>
> Before I can even start on a design, research has to be carried out into what the customer wants and what will sell. I can't always please myself, as economics comes into it as well. Sometimes the fabric I choose is just too expensive to be used.
>
> I love going to fashion shows to get new ideas, and to see if there are any designs I could adapt. Once I have an idea, I try it out by drawing sketches, sometimes using the computer to help me, and also by draping fabrics over a dummy to see how they hang. Seeing my idea being translated into a finished product is really exciting.'

EDUCATION AND TRAINING

There are many full-time courses offered throughout the country, leading to a BTEC National/Advanced GNVQ, a Higher National Diploma or a degree. Entry requirements vary:

minimum entry for a BTEC National Diploma/Advanced GNVQ is usually four GCSEs at grade C or an Intermediate GNVQ, while an HND/degree course will usually need at least one A level plus a foundation course, or a BTEC National Diploma/Advanced GNVQ. Part-time courses are offered in areas of the country where the clothing industry is strong.

Other courses relevant to careers in the fashion industry include marketing, promotion, business and finance, and textile engineering. Look at higher education reference books and the ECCTIS computer database for more information.

just THE JOB

TEXTILE DESIGN

> Textile designers produce designs for a wide range of products, from dress and curtain fabrics to carpets and rugs. As well as being creative, these designers need a good technical understanding of how materials are produced.

Designs can be *printed* on the surface of a fabric (cotton dress materials), or *woven* into it (suit fabrics and tweeds). In producing a design, the designer must take into account the use to which the fabric will be put. Furniture coverings must be tough; curtaining and dress fabrics must drape well. Different colours and motifs will be used for indoor or outdoor clothing, for menswear or baby clothes. Fashion trends in patterns and colours also influence the designs, and manufacturing techniques and costs have to be taken into account.

Woven and knitted fabrics depend for their appearance on the type of yarn used. A designer must have a good eye for colour, and a thorough understanding of the processes used in making and finishing the material. Design is limited to a great extent by what the machines can do. In the design of woven and knitted fabrics, there is a high degree of specialisation and designers concentrate on a few kinds of fabrics. Rough drawings are made by the designer, and sample pieces of fabric are woven from these. The designer may be closely involved with the experimental weaving at this early stage.

The designer of **printed fabric** must know a lot about the various printing processes used, including block, stencil, roller and silkscreen. Flower and plant motifs are popular in printed fabrics, and the ability to draw botanical forms is a very useful skill.

In **carpet design**, a knowledge of looms and the fabrics they can produce is essential background knowledge. Some carpet designs are custom-made – e.g. for cinemas, large firms, hotels and so on. Designers liaise closely with customers, discussing patterns, colour schemes, the furniture to be used with the carpet, etc. Designers of carpets may start as **copyists** setting out designs on squared paper, and colouring the squares to represent individual tufts of wool in the finished carpets. When they proceed to designing, they will make initial sketches and begin the translation of the design onto squared paper, but then pass it on to copyists for completion. In carpet design, knowledge and appreciation of natural forms (flowers, leaves, etc) and of classical ornamentation and period designs is especially useful.

EDUCATION AND TRAINING

There are specialist courses offered by a number of colleges and universities. These are awarded with BTEC National Diplomas/Advanced GNVQs, HNDs or BA degrees. The entry requirement for a BTEC National Diploma/Advanced GNVQ is usually four GCSEs at grade C. Degree courses often require applicants to have completed an art foundation course (minimum entry one A level plus four or five GCSEs at grade C, or the equivalent – most students have more than the bare minimum). The BTEC National Diploma/Advanced GNVQ is more usually followed by a BTEC Higher National Diploma, but progression to a degree is equally possible. All course applicants need a good art and design portfolio.

As well as the entry requirements for courses, you will need to consider the various options available – for instance, printed textiles, general textile design, woven textiles, carpet/rug design, weave/tapestry, knitted textiles, and so on. Details of these will be found in *Design Courses*, published annually by Trotman.

Besides art- and design-oriented courses, there are also courses in textile technology, where the bias is more towards production methods than design. Additionally, there are courses leading to the Associateship of the Textile Institute for which scholarships may be available (details from the Institute – see Further Information section).

It is also possible to follow a course where business studies subjects are taken alongside textile options. These include degrees in textiles management and marketing and BTEC Higher National Diploma courses in business studies with a textile merchandising option.

just THE JOB

GOOD AT NEEDLEWORK?

> There are many jobs and careers which appeal particularly to people with an interest in needlework, fabrics and textiles, dress and fashion. Some of the jobs require ability in needlework (sewing, embroidery or whatever); for others, an interest in the design of textiles, fabrics and dress is the important factor (see previous sections on fashion and textile design). There are opportunities at all levels of qualification.

Fashion/clothing manufacture and other industries using sewing techniques

There are jobs in the manufacturing side of the fashion and clothing industry at all levels, from cutting, sewing machining, pressing and other production processes, up to supervisory and managerial posts. You could work in the production of all kinds of garments – dresses, lingerie and corsetry, outdoor wear, sportswear, men's and children's clothing, and so on. There are also jobs in other manufacturing industries which use sewing as part of the construction process, such as upholstery, household linen, soft furnishings and soft toys.

Sewing machinists and other workers are normally trained on-the-job, and some workers such as cutters may undergo an apprenticeship. There may be other opportunities of employment with training. Supervisory posts are usually filled by experienced production workers. For management positions, there are various specialist training courses available, including those in textile technology mentioned above.

Fashion and other specialist journalism

Fashion journalism is a specialised form of writing for women's pages in newspapers, for the periodicals and women's magazines where fashion features are a high priority, and for the 'style' magazines which are only concerned with fashion. Some newspapers and magazines employ fashion illustrators.

There are also specialist periodicals dealing with other aspects of needlework, crafts and embroidery, which employ expert columnists, either on their staff or on a freelance basis. Magazines frequently have features on dressmaking, making soft furnishings, patchwork, toymaking, knitting and so on. These writers have probably trained originally as home economists or teachers and have moved into journalism as a second career or extra activity.

Embroidery

Machine embroidery is used extensively in the fashion industry for dresses, lingerie, children's wear, etc. Most designing is done by people who have taken special courses in embroidery design at art college. Various courses in embroidery are offered at the London College of Fashion, but these do not attract mandatory awards. These courses train you to design for industrial embroidery within the limitations of the machinery used in industry. It is also possible to take embroidery as a specialist option on a number of BA Art and Design degree courses and BTEC courses at art colleges and universities. These are largely art-biased courses with a highly creative content.

Creative embroidery has very few career outlets. Embroiderers may sell their work to art or craft shops, or carry out commissioned work, but this would rarely be a full-time occupation. It might be combined with teaching or running a needlecraft retailing business, for example. A limited amount of hand embroidery is done for items like banners and ceremonial robes. This work does not generally involve designing, since embroiderers work to the specifications of their customers or to traditional designs. The Embroiderers' Guild offers help with the development of personal work through the Embroiderers' Development Scheme. Each year, the Royal School of Needlework offers three-year apprenticeships in embroidery, as well as a one-year fee-paying part-time certificate course.

Stage and TV costumes

Design of costumes for stage and TV is often a combination of design, dressmaking and historical research. Theatre or TV costume design is highly competitive and there is scope only for the exceptionally talented. Stage costumes need to be tough so that they will last. For films and TV, durability is not usually so important, but costumes must look right on camera. The designer of the show usually produces designs, while theatrical costume designers fill in details and supervise the making. There are a number of two-year DipHE and HND courses, and three-year degree courses in costume design, for which you would receive a mandatory grant. There are also many one- or two-year lower-level certificate or diploma courses, as well as post-graduate qualifications.

Besides posts for designers, there are also jobs for wardrobe assistants and dressers.

Vicky – costume archive director, Paris Opera

My job working with theatre costumes, in Paris, sounds pretty glamorous, and of course, in some ways it is. I do get to see all the new productions and meet directors and artists and go on foreign visits to see costume archives in other countries.

My job is based in the costume store, which is out in the suburbs and not part of the huge and prestigious new

Opera Bastille in the middle of Paris, so my working day starts with a long ride on the Metro. We have all the costumes for the ballet going back for many years, so the job is partly maintaining the archive as well as servicing revivals of more recent productions.

One very interesting job I had to do recently was to research the costumes for a ballet last performed in the twenties by the Ballets Russes. All I had to work on were the reviews of the period, some black and white photographs and the memories of some very elderly dancers about colours and materials. I ended up tracking down a few of the original costumes which had survived and finished up in a collection in England.

Unlike the rather insecure nature of theatre work in the UK, I am a French civil servant, with all the advantages in terms of job security, holidays and pensions that this status involves.

I was very lucky to get started in this work. I had an art college training in England and moved to France to get married. After having a child I wanted to get back to work and did a training scheme involving costume work. A friend working with the Opera suggested I did some work experience with the company and this, very fortunately, led to a permanent job doing practical work in the costume archive. I have gradually worked my way up to my current post as my experience and knowledge have grown. Naturally I have to speak French well. I now find that my English has started to get a bit strange as I catch myself translating French expressions directly into English.

Teaching needlecraft/dress and design

Needlecraft can be taken as the main study on courses leading to a Bachelor of Education degree. Needlecraft is taught in secondary schools by specialist teachers: nowadays, boys as well as girls are taught some needlecraft. Career opportunities for teachers of needlecraft may be comparatively limited. Needlecraft is also taught in colleges of further education, but, apart from leisure classes, this type of teaching is generally done by people with industrial experience. Embroidery and handcrafts are often taught within art departments in colleges.

Retailing

Work at all levels in clothing shops and department stores is one way to involve yourself in fashion. A good sales assistant takes an interest in fashion and is able to help customers find suitable styles. At management level, it is vital to know what lines are likely to sell well in a particular season. For both sales assistants and retail managers, the usual way to train is mainly on-the-job, since individual retailing organisations like to train staff in their own style. It is, however, possible to take part-time courses at many colleges of further education.

The **buyer** in retailing selects the fashion to be stocked by a store. In big firms, this is often a head office job; in smaller businesses, it may be a departmental head's job. There is a BTEC Higher National Diploma in Business Studies with a Retail Fashion Buying option at the London College of Printing and the Distributive Trades.

Display artists or **window dressers** must also have a feel for fabrics and fashions in order to display garments attractively. There are similar jobs in fabric and haberdashery retailing.

Interior design

The work of interior designers concerns the detailed planning of domestic, hotel, office and other interiors. They need to have an interest in fabrics, since the choice of soft furnishings, upholstery and carpets is often an important part of the task.

Dressmaking, alterations, curtain and loose-cover making

Individuals who are skilled at dressmaking can work on a self-employed basis from home, advertising locally for work. Some shops or firms employ people to alter garments, or perhaps make curtains and cushions. Shops specialising in bridal wear, for example, undertake alterations. You need to be highly skilled at cutting and sewing and, unless employed by one firm, would also have to cope with bookkeeping and all the other aspects of working for yourself.

just
**THE
JOB**

WORKING IN THE CLOTHING INDUSTRY

> The clothing industry includes small garment manufacturers, where two or three people work in a room above a shop, large factories with the latest technology, sited on industrial estates and employing hundreds of people, and all the sizes of business in between. Opportunities exist across a wide range of activities within the industry, requiring people with anything from a few GCSEs to a degree.

This section covers the many aspects of work you will find in the clothing industry. You won't find all these jobs in every local firm, as some firms just undertake part of the whole process of garment manufacture. Let's look at the jobs in the order in which they are involved in the making of a garment.

Designer

Designers think up ideas for the manufactured garments. They may produce the patterns and grade them to the different sizes needed. In a large company, this task is often performed by a specialist pattern maker. To be a good designer, you must have a flair for design, and a practical knowledge and experience of production methods. People tend to see the job of designer as the most glamorous in the industry – working on high fashion women's garments for the Paris shows. While that is the work of a very few top designers, most designers are employed by manufacturers designing everyday knitwear, menswear, hosiery and corsetry, etc. Designers usually have a specialist qualification in fashion at Higher National Diploma or degree level, which would take a minimum of two years to achieve through full-time study.

Materials buyer

Buyers have the responsibility for calculating quantities, and ordering the materials necessary to make up newly designed garments in all the different grades or sizes.

Stockroom worker

Their work involves receiving deliveries of materials like cloth, trimmings, buttons and thread. These must be checked against the manufacturer's invoice and stored in a methodical way, so that they can be supplied to other staff for use in producing the goods. The job may also involve noting which items have been used, and re-ordering stock as necessary – possibly using a computerised stock record system.

Cutter and lay planner

Cutters are very skilled workers. They use patterns, produced in the design section, to cut out pieces of material which can then be sewn together to make the garment. Cutters usually work standing up at a large table.

The first step is to arrange a roll of cloth, known to the trade as a 'piece', in layers on a long table. This pile or 'lay' may be many centimetres thick. The process of 'laying-up' may be done by hand or with machinery. Then the pattern is arranged on the cloth so that it can be cut. This is done by the **lay planner**. The pieces of fabric must match up properly when sewn together, and fabric must not be wasted. Computers are often used in this process. Accuracy is very important. The plan may be drawn on paper and attached to the lay, or marked directly on the cloth with chalk or paint. Cutters use hand-held electric cutters, knives or a large stationary cutter – a band knife around which cloth is moved. Another method used is diecutting, where the fabric is cut by a press. The blades of the machine are set according to the lay plan and the press is then lowered on to the fabric to cut the pattern right through the lay.

Training as a cutter can take up to four years as an apprentice or as a trainee under a skilled cutter. This could make it difficult for an adult to get started. Qualifications are not essential but may be required by individual employers. NVQs at levels 1 and 2 in spreading and cutting are available. Arithmetic is important, as are practical skills and the ability to visualise in three dimensions. Cutters need good eyesight and a steady hand. You could eventually progress to cutting room foreman/woman or manager, or move into the more specialised field of master-pattern cutting.

Bundling or dividing

This job involves sorting the cut pieces produced by the cutters, so that the sewing machinists can be given the correct pieces from which to assemble a part or whole garment. Pieces may be numbered to show what they are, and the positions of shaping darts, buttons or buttonholes may be marked. It's important to be careful and methodical. To keep machinists supplied with work, these bundles may be put on a conveyor belt, or taken to machinists by a messenger. If you are alert, good at organising, and want to move around for most of the day, you could enjoy this work.

Sewing machinist

Sewing machinists can work as part of a team, each one making up just a part of a garment – such as the sleeves, or collar – or, occasionally, whole articles. The trend is now for the team to take responsibility for completing whole garments. The machinists no longer work on one single operation and so have to be multi-skilled and more flexible than in the past. Careful, accurate work must be done at speed, and there are many techniques to learn. Full training is given by most firms. NVQs at levels 1 and 2 in stitching are available (see next section).

Hand sewer

Hand sewers may also be employed in the clothing industry. Hand sewing is part of the finishing process, especially for expensive garments, and may involve hemming or finishing trimmings. You need to enjoy doing fine work and to have good eyesight.

Presser

As each item is sewn, it must be pressed, so that seams lie flat and the finished appearance is good. This may involve using a hand iron or a power press. The work requires care and patience, and involves standing for most of the day in a warm atmosphere. Pressers (or formers, as they are sometimes known) can gain accreditation through NVQs at levels 1 and 2.

Examiner

Garments must be checked for quality before they leave the factory or workroom. Poorly made garments won't give the manufacturer a good reputation with wholesalers and retailers. Some checking is done by staff and supervisors as the garment is being produced, and the finished article is given a final inspection. This is done by a trained and experienced examiner. Attention to detail and the ability to make a quick but thorough inspection are important in quality control.

Packing and despatch work

This involves boxing or packaging articles for distribution to a warehouse or shop. Some people working in this department do simple clerical work, noting the numbers of items produced and their destinations. There may be training in employment opportunities for young people.

Supervisor

Supervisors are experienced people whose job is to organise the work of a section or department. This is a post which skilled operators, starting as school-leavers, could reach in their twenties. Later it could lead to more senior management positions. To work as a supervisor, you must be able to assist in the training of your staff. You will be responsible for the quality of work produced in your section, and for the amount of work produced. You must be able to develop a good working relationship with staff and senior management.

Specialist areas of work

There are also opportunities for people to be employed in work requiring specialist techniques and skills, or managerial abilities:

Making hats (millinery) can involve all the skills already described. It may also involve stretching pieces of felt over a metal or wooden hat shape, known as the 'block' and using a steam press to shape the hat. Machining, hand sewing and finishing are important parts of this trade.

Glove and bag making may involve specialising in cutting and sewing leather. Other goods are made of synthetic materials, such as PVC, which may be welded together.

Bespoke tailoring is a very small part of the industry, producing individual garments, suits, overcoats and uniforms which are made to measure. Menswear forms the bulk of the business, though some made-to-measure ladies' garments may be ordered. An experienced tailor would advise customers on fabrics and styles, measure a customer and draft a pattern. Most of the sewing is done by hand rather than machine. It is a highly skilled trade requiring meticulous attention to detail, good eyesight and nimble fingers. Employers usually prefer entrants with GCSEs in English, mathematics and art. Training through an apprenticeship lasts up to five years. Part-time study leading to City & Guilds qualifications in Craft Training and Bespoke Tailoring are available at some colleges of FE. NVQs can be gained in Handcraft Tailoring.

Engineering and technology play an important role in the clothing industry, with opportunities for people at all levels. An assistant mechanic would be responsible for routine maintenance work involving oiling, changing needles and basic repairs to the more common types of machines. Service engineers are employed by sewing machine manufacturers and visit many different firms. As an engineer, you would probably service semi-automatic machines, such as buttonholers and button-sewers. Adapting machinery to cope with new-fabrics and styles might be part of your job. You could also be responsible for the work of several assistants. For entry to these jobs, numerical and practical ability is essential. You may also need GCSE passes in mathematics, English and a science subject. You may be required to do block release study at a college for a BTEC National and, perhaps, Higher National Certificate, but most of your training would be on-the-job.

Trainee technicians and technologists would need at least a few GCSEs, certainly a grade C in mathematics and a physical science. There are opportunities for those with A level, BTEC National or Advanced GNVQ. Entry after a degree or HND is also an option. You might be employed in one of the larger factories where the most advanced machinery is used. Your job could include selecting and maintaining this machinery and designing machine attachments. There are also opportunities for technologists to work for the manufacturers of textile machinery. This is rapidly becoming more sophisticated, as automated systems are being introduced into the larger firms within the clothing industry. Part-time further education for BTEC

National and possibly Higher National qualifications is essential for any young people wishing to make this their career.

Training instructors are usually chosen from the skilled workforce. They analyse the skills needed to do a job and devise training programmes for the staff. They need to know how to operate the machines and must also develop good communication skills, as they may work with everyone in the firm from the newest recruit to the manager.

Management opportunities exist for graduates and for school- or college-leavers (usually with at least A levels or the equivalent, or a BTEC Higher National Certificate) to work in buying, purchasing, sales, marketing, personnel and many other fields. The University of Ulster offers a four-year degree course in Management Studies (Clothing), a year of which is spent in the clothing industry. Other universities offer clothing as an option within business management degree courses.

SEWING MACHINIST

About 70 per cent of the clothing industry's workforce are sewing machinists. They work in factories, workshops and the alteration rooms of shops and stores. Some firms are very small, with only five or six machinists. Really big firms may have 500! There are no formal qualifications required to start as a machinist, but you can gain qualifications while you work.

What machinists do

Machinists sit working at sewing machines. Usually their work is brought to them. Often, each machinist sews or seams just one part of something more complicated. It might be the waistband on a pair of jeans, the straps of lingerie, or the sleeves of a dress. They may also oversew seams to stop them fraying, put in zip fasteners, or do machine embroidery. Besides garments, machinists may work on curtains, stretch covers for furniture, tents, shoes or anything else stitched.

Nowadays, more and more machinists work in small teams which have the responsibility for completing whole garments. This practice makes the work more interesting and allows the machinists to become multi-skilled. They can then be assessed for a variety of NVQs, e.g. in industrial stitching at levels 1 and 2, which can open up more job possibilities.

Industrial machines are basically like home sewing machines, but they are much more solid and faster. They may have computer controls on them, to do a set of operations which are repeated over and over again.

The machinists operate the machines with foot controls. Before starting to sew, they must set up the machines, load the thread and set the stitch length and tension. From time to time, they have to clean the machine, removing dust and ends of thread. As each piece of work is completed, they may do finishing – cutting off spare material and loose threads, and slitting button-holes.

What it takes

This could be the job for you if:

- you don't mind staying in one position all day, whether sitting down or standing at a machine;
- you're good with your hands;
- you don't mind sometimes doing the same thing over and over again;
- you can work quickly – often your pay depends on how much work you get through;
- you can put up with breathing in the fluff and dust which comes off material;
- you have good eyesight;
- you like working in a team;
- you don't mind a noisy workplace.

GETTING STARTED

There are no special entry qualifications, but it is likely to be helpful if you have used a sewing machine before. Both young people and adults are taken on as trainees. There may be opportunities for school-leavers to find training through their local TEC Youth Credits scheme.

You are usually trained on-the-job, by the firm you work for.

There may be a special training room, or you may start at a machine in the normal workroom. Trainees start on simple sewing jobs. Then, with additional training, they can move on to more difficult tasks.

PROSPECTS

With experience, you might become a supervisor, a checker or a quality control inspector. It is also possible to become a sample machinist working in the design department of a factory, making up new designs. This means assembling prototype garments from start to finish.

There are opportunities in machining for part-time work. Some firms also offer outwork, whereby machinists work at home. This can be useful for people who are housebound for any reason, but rates of pay are often very poor.

JUST THE JOB

TEXTILES PRODUCTION

> Any material made with natural or man-made fibres can be described as a textile. The raw starting materials could be cotton, wool, jute, silk, flax, nylon, polyester, etc. These are spun, dyed, woven, knitted and printed to make a tremendous variety of products. Opportunities exist at all levels, ranging from those requiring little or no formal qualifications to degree level and beyond.

Think of a conveyor belt in a factory, a trampoline, heavy jute matting, a sterile wound dressing, a mainsail for a racing dinghy, a silk shirt and a pair of tights: they are all made from textiles. The materials used are made in different ways, by different processes, but they all have one thing in common; they are made in factories by mechanised methods.

Traditionally, certain parts of the country have specialised in particular textiles and have developed highly skilled and experienced workforces. Woollen material fabrics were produced in Yorkshire and the West Country, linen in Northern Ireland, cottons in Lancashire, lace in Nottinghamshire, knitted products in Leicestershire. These areas (except the West Country) are still important, but the development of synthetic materials, like nylon and polyester, and the increase of cheap imports, have brought change to the industry.

The use of computers in design and production has also made great changes, bringing about reductions in the workforce and the closure of out-of-date plant. This has, however, brought an accompanying revival in the profitability and success of the industry. The textile and clothing industries together employ over half a million people.

Most textile firms specialise in some aspects of textile production – e.g. spinning, weaving, dyeing or finishing.

Working conditions can be hot, steamy and dusty. Sufferers

from asthma or other chest complaints may find this causes problems. Some jobs require good colour vision.

Production worker or operative

These people do the basic jobs in the textile industry, operating the fast-moving and noisy machines which produce yarns and fabrics, and carrying out such jobs as cutting, sewing, packing and warehousing. Operatives may not need any academic qualifications, but do need to be quick and good with their hands. At many textile industrial centres, operatives can now work towards National Vocational Qualifications at levels 1 and 2.

Craftsman/woman

Craftsmen and women do skilled jobs which require more training. City & Guilds examinations are available. Craft-level workers may work on the setting up and maintenance of the complex machinery used in the industry, and use specialised hand skills on the textiles themselves.

Technician

Technicians are involved in quality control, design and development, dyeing, printing and finishing processes, as well as work on complex machinery. They may also be supervisors in some areas of the industry. They work under the direction of technologists and managers, and have quite a high level of responsibility. Their training can last for four years or more and involves taking BTEC National and Higher National Certificate courses or textile technician NVQ level 3. Technician apprentices entering the industry would normally need four GCSEs at grade C, including mathematics, a science and one subject showing use of English. Advanced GNVQ in manufacturing with a textiles option may prove a useful starting point. Apprentices who do well in the BTEC examinations and show aptitude can move on to the technologist level.

Technologist

Technologists are responsible for the overall running of factories. They research and develop new products, supervise the commissioning and installation of machinery, and make decisions about all the many highly technical processes involved in spinning, weaving, dyeing and finishing. Technologists are often graduates in specialised subjects such as textile science, technology or engineering, applied chemistry (colour or polymers) or textile management and economics. Sponsorships are available from some of the larger employers in clothing and textiles, e.g. Marks and Spencer. Some may have taken science or engineering degrees and then postgraduate qualifications. With GCSEs or equivalent, it is also possible to enter the industry at technician level and become a technologist through part-time study. The Textile Institute and the Society of Dyers and Colourists confer further professional qualifications, and also publish a list of institutions offering courses relating to textiles and the coloration industry.

Commercial jobs

As well as the technical jobs there are also, as in any industry, many commercial jobs in such areas as marketing, sales, advertising, finance, personnel and so on.

Design

Textile design is a very specialised activity. Before creating a design, the designer must understand the processes involved in producing a textile, in order to know what is and is not possible (see earlier section).

just THE JOB

WORKING IN THE ENTERTAINMENT BUSINESS

> There are many jobs behind the scenes in theatre, film and television, all essential to the success of a production. The particular jobs associated with the theme of this book involve work with costumes and make-up.

The rates of pay for this type of work are variable. Most technical jobs in the theatre are not particularly well paid, but film and television are more profitable. Unfortunately, they are more precarious as well. The majority of technicians rely on the large amounts of essential overtime to boost their earnings. Working hours are long and involve much evening and some night work. You will find below a short description of the jobs and some information on training, but further research (see Further Information section) will be necessary to gather more detailed information. Any experience you can gain in amateur theatre productions is always useful.

Dresser

The dresser looks after wigs and costumes, helps actors dress for the performance and generally assists them. A dresser could combine this job with being a wardrobe assistant. Dressers are not necessarily trained (but see wardrobe master/mistress below).

Wardrobe master/mistress

This involves making, altering and maintaining the costumes. In a rep theatre, the job also involves looking after the costume store, which can be quite large. The work can be very pressured, with deadlines which must be met. Practical skills are very important, particularly the ability to translate drawings into a finished product. A good knowledge of materials is required. There are full-time BTEC HND and degree courses, BTEC National and college diploma courses at many theatre schools.

Wardrobe assistant

Wardrobe assistants help with the routine sewing, ironing and cleaning of costumes. A wardrobe assistant must have good practical skills and be quick and flexible.

Costume designer

The costume designer designs and superintends the costume for the production. He/she decides whether costumes should be newly made, hired or modified from stock. The job does not usually include the practical work of sewing, but it is concerned with producing the working sketches and drawings for the wardrobe department. A designer needs to be able to research costumes of different times and places as well as producing creative solutions for modern period works. A course in fashion design would provide a useful background. Alternatively, there are specialist courses in costume design and theatre wardrobe offered by the London School of Fashion, Rose Bruford College or the Wimbledon School of Art, among others.

Make-up

In theatre, actors generally do their own make-up, so opportunities for make-up assistants may be few and far between. However, make-up artists, working in the theatre in another capacity, may be called upon for advice. There are more opportunities in television and film. Several FE colleges offer diploma courses in theatrical make-up, or it may be included as an option in more general beauty and make-up courses.

FOR FURTHER INFORMATION

GENERAL

See the Laser *Compendium of Higher Education* for details of HND courses, and the CRAC *Directory of Further Education* for other courses. You can also contact the organisations below. The ECCTIS 2000 CD-ROM lists all higher and further education courses in the UK.

BEAUTY

International Health and Beauty Council – 46 Aldwick Road, Bognor Regis, West Sussex PO21 2PN. Tel: 01243 842064.

Working in Beauty, Fitness and Hairdressing, published by COIC.
Careers in Hairdressing and Beauty Therapy, published by Kogan Page.

There are a good many private schools and colleges in all parts of the country. They often advertise in health and beauty magazines and you could also look in *Yellow Pages*.

RETAILING

British Shops and Stores Association – Middleton House, 2 Main Road, Middleton Cheney, Banbury, Oxfordshire OX17 2TN. Tel: 01295 712277.
Distributive Industries Training Trust – 5 Bridge Street, Bishop's Stortford, Hertfordshire CM23 2JU. Tel: 01279 506125.
National Retail Training Council – Bedford House, 69–79 Fulham High Street, London SW6 3JW. Tel: 0171 371 5021.

HAIRDRESSING

BBC Corporate Recruitment Service – PO Box 7000, London W12 7ZY. Tel: 0181 752 4627.

Film and Television Freelance Training (FT2) – 4th Floor, 5 Dean Street, London W1V 5RN. Tel: 0171 734 5141.

Guild of Hairdressers – c/o The Syndicate Group of Companies, Syndicate House, 27/29 Westgate, Barnsley S70 2DJ. Tel: 01226 297083.

Hairdressing Council – 12 David House, 45 High Street, South Norwood, London SE25 6HJ. Tel: 0181 771 6205.

Hairdressing Employers' Association – 10 Coldbath Square, London EC1R 5HL. Tel: 0171 833 0633.

Hairdressing Training Board – 3 Chequer Road, Doncaster DN1 2AA. Tel: 01302 342837.

International Therapy Examination Council Ltd – James House, Oakelbrook Mill, Newent, Gloucestershire GL18 1HD. Tel: 01531 821875.

National Hairdressers Federation – 11 Goldington Road, Bedford MK40 3JY. Tel: 01234 360332.

Vocational Awards International – 46 Aldwick Road, Bognor Regis, West Sussex PO21 2PN. Tel: 01243 842064 (incorporates the International Health and Beauty Council).

World Federation of Hairdressing and Beauty Schools – PO Box 367, Coulsdon, Surrey CR5 2TP. Tel: 01737 551355 – for information on private schools.

TRICHOLOGY

Institute of Trichologists – 228 Stockwell Road, Brixton, London, SW9 9SU. Tel: 0171 733 2056. (Write, enclosing a stamped addressed envelope.)

For addresses of local clinics and practitioners see *Yellow Pages* headings: 'Hair specialists', 'Hair treatment', 'Trichology'. Or you can ask the Institute of Trichologists to give you the name and address of their nearest registered member.

WORK ON CRUISE LINERS

Cunard Line Ltd. – Fleet Personnel Department, South Western House, Canute Road, Southampton SO14 3NR. Tel: 01703 229933.

P&O Cruises Ltd. – Fleet Personnel Department, Richmond House, Terminus Terrace, Southampton SO14 3PN. Send stamped self-addressed envelope for brochure *Seagoing Opportunities with P&O Cruises* for general information, or send letter with cv and stamped addressed envelope for more specific enquiries.

Steiner Group Ltd. – (for hairdressers, beauty therapists, etc) Maritime Division, 57–65 The Broadway, Stanmore, Middlesex HA7 4DU. Tel: 0181 954 6121.

COMPLEMENTARY AND ALTERNATIVE MEDICINE

Association of Reflexologists – 27 Old Gloucester Street, London WC1N 3XX. Tel: 01892 512612.

British College of Naturopathy & Osteopathy – Frazer House, 6 Netherhall Gardens, Hampstead, London NW3 5RR. Tel: 0171 435 6464 – four-year full-time course leading to registration.

General Council and Register of Herbalists – 18 Sussex Square, Brighton BN2 5AA. Tel/fax: 01243 267126.

Institute for Complementary Medicine – PO Box 194, London SE16 1QZ. Tel: 0171 237 5165 – is responsible for the British Register of Complementary Practitioners and publishes an information sheet. Send a stamped self-addressed envelope, together with two loose stamps and a note of which discipline you require information on.

International Federation of Aromatherapists – Stamford House, 2–4 Chiswick High Road, London W4 1TH. Tel: 0181 742 2605.

International Society of Professional Aromatherapists – Hinckley and District Hospital, The Annexe, Mount Road, Hinckley, Leicestershire LE10 1AG. Tel: 01455 637987.

National Institute of Medical Herbalists – 56 Longbrook Street, Exeter EX4 6AH. Tel: 01392 426022.

Reflexologists Society – 39 Prestbury Road, Cheltenham GL52 2PT. Tel: 01242 512601.

School of Phytotherapy (Herbal Medicine) – Bucksteep Manor, Bodle Street Green, Near Hailsham, East Sussex BN27 4RJ. Tel: 01323 833812/4.

Society of Teachers of Alexander Technique – 20 London House, 266 Fulham Road, London SW10 9EL. Tel: 0171 351 0828 (stamped, addressed envelope with enquiries).

The Shiatsu Society – 31 Pullman Lane, Godalming, Surrey GU7 1XV. Tel: 01483 860771.

Vocational Awards International Ltd – 46 Aldwick Road, Bognor Regis, West Sussex PO21 2PN. Tel: 01243 842064. Incorporates the International Institute of Health and Holistic Therapies, which offers diplomas and NVQs in aromatherapy, reflexology and therapeutic massage.

Working in Complementary and Alternative Medicine, by Loulou Brown, published by Kogan Page.

MODELLING

Association of Model Agents – The Clockhouse, St. Catherine's Mews, Milner Street, London SW3 2PX. Tel: 0891 517644. Send a stamped addressed envelope for list of addresses.

London College of Fashion – 20 John Prince's Street, London W1M 0BJ. Tel: 0171 514 7400.

Careers in Fashion, published by Kogan Page (includes modelling).
Working in Fashion, published by COIC (includes modelling).

FASHION

London College of Fashion – 20 John Prince's Street, London W1M 0BJ. Tel: 0171 514 7400.

Design Courses, published by Trotman, contains details of colleges offering fashion design courses at all levels.
Fashion and Textile Design, a booklet about graduate opportunities, is available from Central Services Unit, Crawford House, Precinct Centre, Manchester M13 9EP.
Directory of Further Education, published by CRAC, for information on part-time courses.
Degree Course Guide: Art and Design, published by CRAC.
Careers in Fashion, published by Kogan Page.

Creative Futures: Guide to Courses and Careers in Art, Craft and Design, available from the National Society for Education in Art and Design, The Gatehouse, Corsham Court, Corsham, Wilts SN13 OBZ. Tel: 01249 714825.

CLOTHING AND TEXTILES

British Apparel Centre – 5 Portland Place, London WIN 3AA. Tel: 0171 636 7788.

British Hat Guild – The Business Centre, Kimpton Road, Luton LU2 OLB. Tel: 01582 23456.

CAPITB Trust – 80 Richardshaw Lane, Pudsey, Leeds LS28 6BN. Tel: 0113 239 3355. This is the training organisation and accrediting body for the industries which manufacture products from textiles. Its comprehensive careers pack, entitled *Head to Toe*, may be available at your local careers service.

Confederation of British Wool Textiles – Merrydale House, Roydsdale Way, Bradford BD4 6SB. Tel: 01274 652207.

Embroiderers' Guild – Apartment 41, Hampton Court Palace, East Molesey, Surrey KT8 9AU. Tel: 0181 943 1229.

Institute of Home Economics – Hobart House, 40 Grosvenor Place, London SW1X 7AE. Tel: 0171 823 1109.

KLITRA – Knitting, Lace and Narrow Fabrics Industries – 7 Gregory Boulevard, Nottingham NG7 6LD. Tel: 0115 960 5330.

Royal School of Needlework – Apartment 12a, Hampton Court Palace, East Molesey, Surrey KT8 9AU. Tel: 0181 943 1432.

Society of Dyers and Colourists – Perkin House, PO Box 244, 82 Grattan Road, Bradford, West Yorkshire BD1 2JB. Tel: 01274 725138.

Textile Institute – 10 Blackfriars Street, Manchester M3 5DR. Tel: 0161 834 8457. Please write to the Qualifications Officer for specific information about their accredited courses only; they are unable to give general careers information.

THEATRE, FILM AND TELEVISION

Arts Council Drama Department – 14 Great Peter Street, London SW1P 3NQ. Tel: 0171 333 0100.

Association of British Theatre Technicians – 47 Bermondsey Street, London SE1 3XT. Tel: 0171 403 3778.

Film and Television Freelance Training – The Administrator, FT2, 4th floor, 5 Dean Street, London W1R 5RN. Tel: 0171 734 5141.

Spotlight – 7 Leicester Place, London WC2H 7BP. Tel: 0171 437 7631. Publishes *Contacts* – an annual list of information on companies, courses and everything to do with theatre work.

The Stage is a weekly newspaper, available from your newsagent or on subscription from 47 Bermondsey Street, London SE1 3XT. Tel: 0171 403 1818.

British Theatre Directory is a useful source of theatre-related information available from Richmond House Publishing Company, Richmond Mews, London W1V 5AG. Tel: 0171 437 9556. This volume may be held in your local library.

Information on full- and part-time courses in technical theatre subjects can be found in the CRAC *Directory of Further Education*, the Laser *Compendium of Higher Education* and the ECCTIS course database, which may be available in your school, college or careers centre library. You'll need to consult individual college prospectuses to find out full details of the course content. The Association of British Theatre Technicians is currently updating a useful directory of courses and training opportunities in backstage theatre work. In the meantime, they will send a free leaflet on receipt of a stamped addressed C5 envelope.

For set and costume design courses, see *Design Courses,* published by Trotman for the Design Council and available for reference in most careers centres.